THRESHOLD

For Bonnie –
co-conspirator in
poetry –
Fondly –
Jim
October 1998

PHOENIX **POETS**

A SERIES EDITED BY ALAN SHAPIRO

JAMES LONGENBACH

T H R E S H O L D

THE UNIVERSITY OF CHICAGO PRESS

Chicago and London

James Longenbach is Joseph H. Gilmore Professor of English at the University of Rochester. His poems have apperared in many publications, including *The Nation*, *The New Republic*, *The Paris Review*, and *The Best American Poetry 1995*. He is also the author of several critical works, most recently *Modern Poetry after Modernism*.

The University of Chicago Press, Chicago 60637
The University of Chicago Press, Ltd., London
©1998 by The University of Chicago
All rights reserved. Published 1998

07 06 05 04 03 02 01 00 99 98   1 2 3 4 5

ISBN: 0-226-49245-1   (cloth)
        0-226-49247-8   (paper)

Library of Congress Cataloging-in-Publication Data

Longenbach, James
Threshold / James Longenbach.
    p.   cm. — (Phoenix poets)
ISBN 0-226-49245-1 (cloth : alk. paper). — ISBN 0-226-49247-8 (pbk. : alk. paper)
I. Title. II. Series.
PS3562.04967T48 1998
811'.54—dc21   98-10950
CIP

*for Joanna,
Kathryn, and
Alice*

Contents

Acknowledgments

Grateful acknowledgment is made to the editors of the following publications in which these poems, or versions of them, first appeared:

Boulevard: "How to Remember"
Colorado Review: "Elective Cardioversion," "My Other Self"
Denver Quarterly: "Another Person"
The Nation: "A Dog, a Horse, a Rat," © *The Nation*, 1995; "Yard Work,"
    © *The Nation*, 1997
The New Republic: "The Lucky Ones"
The Paris Review: "Bandusia" (as "After Horace"), "Faithless Angel,"
    "The Grace of the Witch," "Letting Go," "Natural World"
    (as "Stories Told about the Natural World"), "The Origin of
    Angels," "Orpheus or Eurydice," "The Possibilities"
    (as "Things You'll Never Know")
Raritan: "The Afterthought," "Burglary" (as "Burglary Considered
    as a State of Mind"), "The Pretty Rocks"
Salmagundi: "Any House You Know," "In a World without Heaven,"
    "Play with Me"
Southwest Review: "Real Estate," "We Are Gathered Here"
The Yale Review: "Answers to a Question," "What You Find in the Woods"
Western Humanities Review: "Threshold of the Visible World"

"What You Find in the Woods"also appeared in *The Best American Poetry 1995*, ed. Richard Howard and David Lehman (New York: Simon and Schuster, 1995).

THRESHOLD

What You Find in the Woods

Nothing in the air to call me here—
Trees recede into the dark circumference
Of the hill and everything's reduced
To the chilled circle of its lesser self.
No muddy spoor, no red sleeve of a fox
Against snow. But things accumulate
As if from nothing. Nests of broken glass.
A frozen mess of feathers, kicked, upturns
The bird intact, the tiny beak a rictus.

Once, when I lived near woods like these,
I followed older boys who stumbled
On a child's body wrapped in wool—nothing
Left but sinew tangled with bones.
What's this? Sycamore bark that's flaked
Away like skin. Trees shift uneasily—
A hawk, wings too lofty for this wood,
Descends to look at me; its head turns once
Before the branch it rests on breaks away.

Then nothing. Silence thinning on a hill
Too low for speculation on our lives—

There's nothing here I don't already know.
So more than anything, more than the slow,
Determined beat of wings, I'm on the lookout
For the bone, the skeleton half buried
In leaves, the body sprinkled hastily
With dirt and sticks, the open hand, the face
Disheveled and no stranger than my own.

Answers to a Question

Why, why do we feel
(we all feel) this sweet
sensation of joy?

Because our being in the world is not
A busride through darkest night unless
We stall midway with our ambivalence,

A stuttering, fortitude disrupted
As wind dispels our diesel spume.
Because no one deserves another home.

Because by asking we convince ourselves
The answer's plain, as children entertain
Themselves with riddles that can't be solved.

Because we've traveled half the way, we know
Joy is not sweet. It is the act of feeling—
The wish that what we feel is shared,

Each of us moving forward in single thought,
The way headlights seem to part the trees
Though we know the road precedes us,

Opening and closing on our solitudes.
Because no one can bear to sit alone.
Because we're terrified by unity, each face

· 5 ·

Concealing what we thought to share.
Because we can't be sure the feeling
Won't be fortified by doubt, a longing

To revoke the question posed—*why*,
Why—these words repeated by a woman
Who appeared once in the middle of the night

To serve me tea, two porcelain cups
With spoons laid neatly at the saucers' rims.
Look, there's the street where we were born!

You by the window, do you feel it now?
And you, the woman with grocery bags
And raincoat folded on her lap, the man

Beside her mumbling incoherently,
The children sleeping or the crying ones
Who will not be consoled? I felt it once:

Ambivalence released me where asphalt
Lapses in a grove of orange trees,
The ocean blue, a body that receives

The body like an offering but seeps
Inside it to dissolve a dark recluse—
The soul's rouged, uncompromising face.

Burglary

It's not the violation but the weight
Of everything left behind: dark clouds
Reciprocate the nothing in your eyes
With the suspicion there's nothing missing
Under surfaces. A finch abandons
What she built in the ailanthus and if
You were a bird you'd leave here too—
Leave all the things not yet accumulated,
One white ribbon dangling from the nest.
Consult the memory for a scene more
Welcoming than this: dawn so scarlet
Off the island, once, you prayed although
You hadn't said a prayer since childhood.
Whatever can't be stolen can't be owned
But even thoughts like these are miserly
And what remains may never be accounted for.
A wine glass found weeks later in the woods.
The telephone, dead when you pick it up,
Sky a thousand different shades of gray—
Hello? *Hello?* Who measures out the value

Of accumulation, who can tell
You when it's gone? Broken window or
A blur of wings above the empty mouths:
Please make a list of everything you own.

Real Estate

1.

The woods are growing and the tallest hickory leans
A little further every summer toward
The clubhouse I've constructed in the eaves.

It's late, television humming me to sleep
But I'm awake, the part of me that never sleeps—
Does not grow old since it was never young,

And as the screen goes blank the hill implodes,
One small protuberance inverting to a dimple
So insignificant no map could mark its place.

Hickories drop their boles and dangle in the pit,
A thousand toothpicks in a row, except for one
Still growing more complete although it falls

Toward almost nothing—all the world I've built
Together with the artifice purchased here,
The whole contraption, septic tank to aerial,

Horsehair plaster slathered on the lath
Collapsing with a sound that if I heard it from
Another planet, I'd have to call a sigh.

2.

Stars, moons, the night sky fabricates itself
More easily than any shelter we've raised
But doesn't satisfy our craving for astonishment.

Not the kind I muster, carrying the baby
From the house across prickly grass, constellations
More imperious than I remember since I held

The cardboard wheel displaying them fleshed,
Explicable, the arbitrary world converted with a spin
Into a playground vision of ascendancy.

Nothing I can tell her, heavy in my arms,
Will make those seven stars cohere into a dipper—
It's a kind of spoon—not because the mind

Refuses to connect the dots, but because the things
That make up heaven don't resemble any
Of the objects in a world she's ever known.

3.

The survey shows that by triangulation, lines
Converging from two corners of the house,
I'll find the spot where downspouts meet

Before they spill the run-off to a sewer rumbling
Beneath the street. And if I'm skilled
Enough to pace the line, patient enough

To dig through roots exfoliating just
Below the surface from hemlocks planted long
Before I walked or spoke, I'll reach the trap—

The rusted elbow suffering half a century
Of what no holder of the deed imagined as neglect
Because no signs of stress were visible:

Water seeping backward through the landfill,
Freezing, thawing, crumbling mortar spread
Between the cinder blocks, a thousand cracks—

The atlas of conceivable astonishment
Unfolding on the basement wall more quickly
(If the lifetime of a house were equal to the planet's)

Than the universe expands.

4.

                    It's *personal*, not *real*,
If the thing itself could never be restored
Once we're dispossessed of our estate; *corporeal*

When what we hold we hold by physical possession,
Incorporeal when what we know is ours
We know by trust, a string of signatures connecting

Us across the planet to a cultivated hillside,
Mottled schist, vintner on hands and knees—
A world from which we benefit but do not tend.

Here, where I can touch the place I live,
Books pressed against ceiling, desk and chair,
Brandy glistening at bedside while the nightmare

Flares its nostrils at my sleeping form,
What's real is an empty shelf, formidable
Until I've filled it, overwhelming once it's full.

We comb the stars in search of emptiness,
A place to begin again—reconstructing,
Rearranging what's thought or found into a space

That isn't distinct from what we own but seems,
Though the law's not on our side, more personal,
More incorporeal than anywhere we've lived before.

Natural World

Two ospreys stir the branches over our heads
And circle the wide water. Cormorants,
The year's first mackerel running in the weeds.
Below the house, the dock collapses in mud,
Pilings snapped by one unnatural tide.
The few pines left across the cove preside
In black against the scorched peninsula.

Even if water could rise, flames never
Could reach us here. But I'm adrift—
An image floats towards me, white as ash.
I think of Baudelaire's rogue swan,
Webbed feet clumsy on the cobblestones,
Beak poked raw. I think of those
Who lose what never can be found again.
The rocks we sit on, nothing more.

Ospreys glide with one eye on the nest
Then slash the air, and like a sledge against wood
They hit the surface of the water,
Silver muscles churning in their talons
As the bodies rise together to the trees.

Somewhere, even while we sleep, the world
Is measuring our share of happiness:
Everything born is nurtured by debts
Of lifetimes spent. Untended, fires thresh
These pines and floods rejuvenate the soil.
A scruff of feathers grows to be a swan.
Salmon spawn, the young survive. We've learned
These stories told about the natural world
And now, dissatisfied, we pass them on.

The Afterthought

Not far from home the river splits
Into a dozen creeks and dead-end spurs.

But I prefer to linger here beside
The long canal boats with painted hulls

And far-fetched names. One night I walked too far.
The towpath dwindled to a slice of land

Between river and barge canal
Until it disappeared, the surface clear,

Uncomplicated as a magpie's caw.
I'd heard of fishermen who never learn

To swim because it's easier imagining
A simple death; I knew that under

Any surface is a maelstrom swirling
With evidence of other people's lives.

I hadn't seen how easily the body
Could forget the skills it brings to water

Cold and indiscriminate as this,
The mind released for just one moment

From a lifetime's weight of loss and grief
Before it sinks more quickly than a stone,

The body following. The afterthought.

Orpheus or Eurydice

For seven days he sat along the bank
In filthy garments stained with river mud.
Indifference, jealousy, or recognition

Makes us disregard what happened next,
How he not only made shrubs and stones
Dance wickedly but dandled shepherd boys

As if no man had ever thought to do so,
Felt delicate beards against his thigh
Until the men of Thrace all took to boys

But not exclusively, long nights home
With the women of Thrace, returning for more,
Never the same way twice. So they pierced

His mouth while he was singing, cheered his head
And lyre floating down the Hebrus,
As so many after him have loved the sound

Of wind in the acanthus and so paid
For what they loved, the slender bodies
Almost indistinguishable from here,

As if no one remembers pale skin
Beneath the bathing suit, fleshy parts
Now hard or soft depending not so much

On what you managed to perform but who it was
Behind that scrim of chlorinated sweat—
The interim between the spastic lull

Of childhood and its mentionable end,
Beside the river or golfcourse or whatever
Margin comes to mind, a body's means

To pleasure is not limited by what the parts,
Or so we learn, have been designed to do.
Music can't be held responsible.

Even sex is not enough to lubricate
The wheels of this narrative, however wayward,
Since behind the ritual dismemberment

The story's more familiar than we recognize:
It doesn't take a trip to hell
And back for us to know transgression,

Carrying the extra sets of clothes
We've worn since childhood, boundaries
And considerations we'd like to drop

Beside the soiled mattress on the floor,
Aware that while transgressing, we also obey.
It's like the message smeared in pencil

On a bathroom wall: the rough-hewn cry,
Backward glance forbidden in the mind—
Uncertain, gentle, and without impatience

As the memory turns to hobble through
The meadow back into the mind's dark core,
Concealing a switchblade or a smile.

The Grace of the Witch

Romance of the twelve-year-old who finds
Himself behind the school in a Stingray,
How he's never the same. I had a friend

Whose father slipped a condom in his hand—
But make her swear, no witches' tricks—a rite
Of passage meaningless to us because

We understood it wasn't ours. One night
We found her at the playground, barefoot,
Floppy hat, frayed jeans dragging

In the dust as she swung back and forth.
Block letters cut into her wrist spelled *Paul*.
There, on our bicycles, street lights

Signaling our time was up, we learned—
It wasn't obvious—she loved him then
So it didn't hurt. I tossed her beads

And eagle feathers when she disappeared,
To where, we couldn't guess, since any house
We knew seemed incapable of breeding her.

In a movie she'd have been the Nazi wife
Who overwhelms the beautiful French soldier,
Underage, who's grateful anyway—

The woman in the woods, long white hands,
Amber honey mixed with wine—*never*
A man that drank this cup but when it passed

His lips he had succumbed—and in her arms
A hairless torso heaving expertly.
We saw her at the beach, or someone like her,

Swimming in her clothes, no underwear,
A bottle hoisted to her lips each time
The water knocked her down. It seemed

Unfair—indecent—that your body would
Display, where everyone could see,
The name of someone you didn't love.

We asked her at the swings—it baffled me—
If she would scrape the scar away. She said,
I'd need a razor. Can you get me one?

Learning to Drown

One loved a rich man, left him,
Followed him to France.
Another tidied up
The family tree by sleeping
With his brother's wife.

You hear these stories told
Of love's first treachery—
A hook, the lair, remembering
The night you found black
Water translucent
From the other side.

One stayed because the road
Was blocked, though he promised
He would walk alone.
One felt the presence
Of her mother in the room.

No one chased you though
You ran until you broke
Yourselves, two bodies
Sprawled in marsh
Grass combed like hair.

One says she hated it.
One woke up huddled
On the bathroom floor.
He wonders if we learn
To suffer, leavening
Ourselves with what we loathe.

You watched a hand float toward
Your face, effortless,
The pond a skin your bodies
Had secreted to replace
The world through which you ran—
Where breathing in, you can't
Not touch the one who dwells
Beside you, brother, twin,
Knowing water wastes
The body, heart and limb,
Realizing what you love
Can't hurt you once you drown.

Tell that to the victim
Says the one who fought
Her father off. She wonders
How a child bears
The story of our lives.

Another Person

for Maureen Howard

We need another person's story to survive.
The boy who drags his arm across the saw

As earth detaches from its moorings,
Lurching in the dark to let him through.

We cannot choose the room in which we're born
But feel cold air rushing to our lungs

And know a world that enters us is better
Than the solitude we've left behind—

The warmth hospitable, but only because the body,
Long before it breathes, creates the space

In which it dwells, maintaining balance,
Lolling, free, luxuriating in a pool

Of its urine. We forget this easily.
A story finds us, and we call it our own,

Counting the rings accumulated year by year,
Wood sanded clean of the catastrophe

And hoisted high above us where the door
Will hang, hinges oiled, swinging free.

The immigrant who ties his only daughter
To the rowboat's spine. She's rescued, blistered

But alive. The widow who consigns
Her husband's body to a pauper's grave

And sells the furniture, two walnut tables
And a painted screen. No purpose has presided

But events create a form, a world of stories
Intersecting, interfering with each other

So they end at different times. Some die, some thrive,
But we create the space in which we dwell

From what another person leaves behind,
Conceiving new ones that provide

Stories of the world before we understood
We ever were alive. And as we tell them,

Moving toward our end, our lives are multiplied:
The body lurches as earth turns over once

To let it through, eyes shut tight, arms flailing
In the atmosphere as if to churn

The world into compliance, howling naked, never free,
A seed that fluttered drowsily

Before it grew into another person
Entering the story in mid ecstasy,

A violation of our solitude,
The unknown new, and ending endlessly.

The Origin of Angels

Everything I've heard about heaven is true.
Italian landscape hazy with the blush
Varnish takes above an egg-wash sky.
Except the faces. Not with parted lips
And golden hair but like a child's face,
Like the one I know, still grimy, unprepared.

Each night, hovering above the shape
That heaves its perfect breaths, hands
Unclenching from an object, lost or found,
No less important for not being there,
I make some useless gesture, smooth a blanket,
Brush my lips against dampened hair:

This is the origin of angels, all
Of providential history turning back
To our first parents, Adam's fingers twisted
In a knot of grief above the silver corpse
As in *The Death of Abel* by Bonnat,
Eve wondering how it could be—

With everything we know about heaven,
That children understand the means
And ends of suffering before their parents do.
It's when I'm on the verge of sleep
That I can see their faces as they scamper
Through a backlit meadow, unaware of me.

Play with Me

Desire for the colloquies
Of make-believe already shrunk
Into a worn, one-sided thrust

Against the understated kiss,
Coffee mingling with toothpaste
In grownup morning protocol:

Play with me. It is the first
Defense against love, the begging
And the holding off, a pretense

Meant to build a world apart
But like all metaphors, teardrop
Dangling from the swollen lid,

Depends on what it leaves behind
Until it falls, the game refused,
And morning broken by a will

Not larger but less practiced
Than our own. We're free to spurn
The inexplicable behavior,

Free to pacify the children
Who'd only failed, or succeeded,
To believe that they were us.

Elective Cardioversion

As if the body were no longer single
But a colony of disparate parts,
As if the center, where the heart once ruled,

Were overtaken by a strange democracy—
Metaphors by which you used to live,
Pump or drumbeat, replaced by similes

That churn inside you like a squirrel.
And to extirpate them you submit
To this too fathomable parody of science,

Remnant of the nineteenth century
Surrounded by machines that can project
The discombobulation of your pulse

In moving pictures while an intern holds
The jellied paddle to your chest, still cold
Before it burns. And in the pause between

Lightning and the thunder crack,
The fuselage before it snaps in two,
Between the blindfold and the hairy noose,

Three hundred joules of what transformed
The primal soup into a wriggling stew
Have thrown you upright so your arms, elastic,

Reach for nothing and your elbows snap,
The ricochet, the brain no longer speaking
With the blood. And in the millisecond

When the screen articulates a vacancy,
The heart awakened from its undulant
Haphazard stream of electrons—call it life—

You are a child fastened to a gurney,
Eyes rolled back, limbs gesticulating
What the mind no longer registers,

Her parents wandering the hall, hearts
Beating faster than a metaphor
Could shape your life before it breaks—

As if, just for the moment when the muscle
Is immobilized, you don't remember
How to love yourself, and by forgetting

Claim her suffering, until the heart,
Despotic, firm, above all, mannerly,
Falls back to sleep, and you survive.

Any House You Know

Somewhere in the grid
Of shingled roofs,
Summer rows
Of browned-out lawns,

One neat, ramshackle
House, not yours,
Collapses slowly
In a burning mire:

It is the oldest fear.
Strangers at the curb.
Smoke that smells
Like seasoned wood,

The kind my father
Saved for holidays.
My neighbor says
She's dreaming

Of a barcalounger
In the Caribbean
Where she'll stretch out
With a stiff one—here.

She holds her hand
As if around a glass
Although it could
Easily be a rope.

Somewhere a child
Disappears in smoke,
Not here, since no one
Bolted for the woods

Convinced what's missing
Could be found.
Plywood fits
The windows perfectly.

Trucks pull out.
The sky clears, blue
As heaven in
A child's drawing—

Crooked chimney,
Family on the stoop.
It could be any
House you know.

Yard Work

It must be human, what we lose
That never can be found again—

A soul, but it's only here,
Stem turned brown, the hose

A listless trickle at my feet,
That I imagine any meaning

For the word, thinking of
A wilderness of stone in Paris

Where a woman lights a candle,
Places it among a hundred

Other flames and watches tears
Of wax congealing on the floor.

I could see there was nothing
For her, not the stone, the candle

Or the flame, no arms that held her,
Cradling her body like a child's—

Nothing that could bring it back,
No matter what she could believe,

No matter how each spring would come
To haunt her, dormant roots,

These tubers sending up a single flag
As if to test the atmosphere,

The shallow light that coaxes
And deceives: *all clear, all clear*.

A Dog, a Horse, a Rat

I look hard for the lights of the city.
Clouds lift from cooling towers as the train
Slows down. A crane hoists bands
Of railroad iron; then the chains hang free.

It is a night for welcoming disaster—
The face at the door that without speaking
Tells you someone's gone. To comprehend
This is the worst would be the only way
To know your feelings on a night like this.

Not far from here a child was beaten on a bet
Or dare and left for dead along the tracks.
A woman saw him in the underpass:
The boy—already dazed and bruised but not
Enough, who clutched the hands of his
Custodians—was frightened of her dog.

I know an actor, playing Lear, who fights
Against the thought of his own daughter
When he holds the body in his arms,

Convinced there's something imprecise
Or even disrespectful in the act
Of feeling more. I'm fighting now.
Why don't we know what to be frightened of?
When should we say *this is the worst?*

It's better that the world stays unaware
Of human feeling on a night like this
Or any night, the tainted clouds, these bands
Of iron crossing endless wooden ties.

The Possibilities

When you were only a possibility,
Long before we imagined that we'd lose
Our way, we stumbled on the fountain

We'd been looking for, the pool dry—
Gods and tritons cracked and thin
Behind a chain-link fence that blurred

Into a veil, like the one that draws us,
Following ourselves, into the past.
Not even Rome makes wishes come true:

Aeneas, mixing ash with wine, surveying
All future generations' gifts to Rome,
Attends to one tall youth, more beautiful

Than any other but with clouded brows
And downcast eyes, the child we will mourn,
For whom lilies offer nothing in return.

It would be useful to believe we'd meet
Again, and all of Christianity
Seems poised against its knowledge

That the one who dies is not the mother
But the child, Jesus railing at heaven
And the sky, unanswering, omnipotent,

The image of what every parent feels
In the face of suffering that nothing
We've learned to do throughout the long,

Unrewarded climb into adulthood
Can assuage. The possibilities
Are burdensome enough to think of

Much less see: snowplow sliding off
The exit ramp or blond hair mimicking
A breezy summer at the bottom of the pool.

We're children then ourselves, incapable
Of action or intelligible speech—
A drooling infant sucking on his hands

Like Ugolino, who must hear his children
Whimper for bread and bear their charity
—*Our pain will lessen, father, if you eat us*—

And do nothing but observe sunlight
Leaking through the grille as one by one
Children dwindle to the floor and die.

We need to rehearse the possibilities
—As if we'd hold them off by conjuring
Our long-lost pleasures, pancakes wide

As dinner plates, served up with confidence
That what worked once may, recreated,
Work again. But even if we pay

The piper once he's rid the town of rats
They follow anyway: children lost,
Abandoned, past all help, all hurting, rise

Into the hills across Rat River where ghosts
Of children never born whisper
Play with me—and we awaken in sweat

And stumble down the corridor to check
Their beds, their breathing, too embarrassed
To admit when we dream about their deaths

We want to die. For if pancakes work,
Piano lessons, weekends at the barn,
Children resurrect the loss, the part of us

That's disappeared: no one, having put
The past to sleep, however nurturing,
However fondly we remember it,

Could want to see its specter wandering
That hallway in the middle of the night
To ask for water or to say *I'm cold*.

You are as fond of grief as of your child,
Says a voice inside us, harsh, uncompromising
As the river where they waved good-bye.

But we retaliate. Like the mother
Who begins to grieve before the prince
Is gone, we play a scene, put on a show:

Grief fills the room of my absent child,
Lies in his bed, walks up and down with me,
And stuffs his vacant garments with his form.

My daughter plays ferociously; I'm not too old
To play along. Before she spoke
I thought I'd come to understand her

Perfectly—as if by listening I'd have
An answer in the middle of the night.
There's one more possibility. We tossed

Some lire in the empty pool and as if
Parched stone could hear us, water burst
From every orifice, the past undone,

And wonder rising through the air like mist.
I don't remember what we wished,
But anything that ever found us was you.

In a World without Heaven

1.

The youngest feels the winter stars receding
As willows raise their skirts and wave good-bye.

She sings herself a lullaby, mimicking
Her sisters' voices until the room is scoured
Of its emptiness.
                  Each night they kissed
Her forehead and unclenched her fists—
Still clinging to the treasure of the day,
Before they fumbled with the light and closed the door.

2.

Time was the sisters swept the floor more neatly
Than their mother had. They strained with rags
Until the window shone more brightly than the moon.

When the youngest cried at night, cried harder
Than they'd cried themselves when she was born,

They stood on ladders, memorized the view
And brought it home.
                              Soon anything they found
Became a gift. As their collection grew
The room became more cluttered than the world.

3.

One night the youngest heard them rise, one voice
Gathering from their bodies as they wept
For little things they'd have to leave behind.

Willows shivered in the wind that swept
The voice beyond the highway's ribbon of stars.
No one could stop.
                              No one could listen
For the youngest who, once they were gone,
Would have to live alone the longest time.

4.

And when she asked about their bodies, sinking
In the ground, the sisters told her of
A mother, larger than their own, who lifts
Them up and teaches them to wave good-bye:

Children bending plump, unpracticed fingers,
Growing younger, smiling sleepily, forgetting
Every face they'd ever loved. The sisters
Didn't believe the story.
                              Nor did she.
The youngest still remembers how
Their bodies felt against her, damp and warm.

5.

The youngest feels days accumulate
Like objects in the room. Days cut and stacked
Like wood waiting to be burnt to ash
And swept away, ashes soft as feathers
On the floor.
                    There's nobody left to give
Things to. The wood is silent, feathers shine—
A bird still opening its beak as if
To let the singing back inside.
                                        Every night
The youngest burns the gifts they left behind.

6.

The room explodes with diamonds in her memory,
A lifetime's worth of fireflies released
From jars where they convinced her they'd died.

But it's only a night like any night, one more
Good-bye, a child rising from the bed
Like a ghost behind the headstone reappearing
To its mother for a final kiss,
                                        a butterfly,
Dark lashes against her cheek at last once more
Before we fumble with the light and close the door.

The Pretty Rocks

Arms of land enclosing open sea,
Focusing wind that ripples up
The meadow to the orchard, mylar kites,
A single heron with its neck extended
So improbably: but in the distance
There's the massive break, a wilderness
Of ocean close enough to witness
But remote enough to let us savor
The millennia of punishment
Rocks can suffer while we sleep.

A child scampers through the meadow,
Waits for recognition from older kids,
Intent on breaking limestone to dust
With granite gathered from the shore.
Two steps towards them, then away, not running
Or retreating but withholding something
Inexplicable, as if her movement
Through the world were nothing but a dull
Reflection of what's happening inside
—Or somewhere else.

                    She won't remember this
But she will understand the feeling,
Windswept arms containing all that water
And the opening or else a closing
Of the ocean far—but not too far—beyond.
The soul, if we remembered how we made it,
Would be similar: the pouring out
And then the violence of the rushing in,
The outside twisted back upon itself
To carve a coastline of interiors,
Caves and mazes, and the refuse
Of construction strewn along the shore.

We're silent, she and I, the world so full
Of nothing but the sound of one rock pounding
On a softer one to make the powder
Sifting into the bucket down below.
Go find the pretty rocks, says one lost child
To another one, and off she goes.

How to Remember

Yellow fields parting in the wind.
Unpaved roads so overgrown with weeds

They brushed against windows on both sides.
An open square. Hours passing undetected

While we played together on the grass,
Three of us, our bodies silhouettes

Against the dusky, cultivated hills.
Foxgloves we held you up to smell—

The distance lost, but only for a moment
As ocean filled the air like smoke.

Could we have known that all the moments
We'd recall would rise like smoke, obscuring

The sight of everything that was?
Could we have found a place where nothing

Can be forgotten since, as each day lifts
Its vast accumulation to the next—

The ruined chapel and the heifers chewing
Silently—there's nothing to forget?

Once, we brought you to a foreign place
And the world we'd seen a hundred times,

Seen by more human eyes than we could count,
Became inscrutable and then grew clear.

It might have been the chapel rising
As we turned along the riverbank.

Rain that washed away our footsteps.
Old stone crumbling back into the sky.

My Other Self

I'm walking where ocean thins to nothing,
Unaware of what I'll leave behind—

The cure I'd find in footprints, shells,
Or better, in morphology

Since there are shells enough but little cure.
No house inhabited that is not paid

And dickered for. No desk arranged
But by an order making sense to someone,

Even disarray. No pillow that won't hide
The stain human effort can't disguise,

No matter if I've scrubbed until
The pattern dwindles and fabric frays,

Accumulating value, in a way—
Nothing to be squandered, lost or saved,

Unless by wandering a harbor so demure,
So manicured it's unaware of how

Elements that made it could dismantle
Any structure, large or small,

I'm loosened from the daily surge
And summoned by a legacy:

A perfect body in a soapy blur—
A hummingbird surveying the submerged

Geography, the small interstices
Between water and rock, distinguishing

The shadows from the solid forms
Until it pierces mine, and disappears.

Faithless Angel

As a child I never bolted, made a scene
Or misbehaved, so every week it seemed
A blank necessity, like waking up

To snow, the boat adrift, or raking leaves.
The lure of worship never reached my soul.
All big ideas, from democracy

To birthday presents, though I practice both,
Never were emptied of their meaning since
I never had a certainty to lose.

Birds don't sing around the bungalow,
They cough, they sputter, congregate and yell.
Maybe if I'd had a dog myself

I'd understand why loose affection seems
To gather in such moments, unforeseen,
Unasked for, like a golden crown descending

On the undeserving pirate's head.
But if I ever entertained the notion
That simple forms of human conjuring

Could mend whatever cosmic rift had made
Us mortal, I discovered long before
My mind was capable of understanding

What acquittal of the body's last
Infirmity could mean, that great books
Belie the longing they've aroused

For immortality and recommend,
Too often smugly, that we all get back
Into the boat, return to Italy,

And like mackerel crowded underneath us
Procreate and die. Our faith is faith
In someone else's faith, said William James,

And watching snow dissolve in the canal,
Dead fish in the window and the waitress
Reappearing with grappa poured

In two small globes, I could believe
In human pleasure; but as many times
As we retraced our steps we never happened

On that restaurant again. It disappeared
Like certainty, a fine ideal—where
In all this moonlit, dream-infested city

Is it found? The body is dogmatic.
It generates belief. We're better off
With anything that leaves us between,

Humanizes indecision so we learn
To recognize the moment we've become,
Too hopelessly, assertively, ourselves.

The faithless angels who did not rebel
Were sentenced to this place—not hell,
Where the condemned would seem more beautiful—

But to a margin, fed on bitter grass,
And forced to wander through frozen marshes,
Unremitting plains, until their footsteps

Cut these channels and their voices raised
Sunburnt palace walls that ask from us
No blessing, no condolence, no reprieve.

Bandusia

Dark vines snaking the hillside where
Sabines lived, where everything slants,
Where a village clings to the hill
As if retreating from a fire.

Where the road still winds deep
In the wood until it disappears:
No gate, no keeper, but a path
Edged neatly with white polished stones.

All lost—the garden and the mask
Of Silenus, mosaics of colored glass,
The fountain's mouth and bones of Christians
Bleached by centuries of light.

But still these steep, unbroken hills
Around us and the fields below.
And here the clearing where the wolf
Once strayed to overhear the song.

Where the path still rises higher
Toward the scent of wintergreen—
Where swallows dart into the chasm,
Turning once, to reappear.

Remember here the modest gift of wine,
Goat's blood, red in icy water
Pouring gently from a cleft in stone
As from an urn tipped carefully

So you can cup your hand beneath
Its flow—now drink, and in its music
Hear the source of its own praise:
The clear-voiced spring of Bandusia.

We Are Gathered Here

Blackbirds scatter from the orange trees.
On ladders, nuns press broken bottle glass
In stucco spooned like frosting on the wall.

Below, an iron slit in stone, no door,
Where gypsies queue with children on their hips.
Lizards scatter in the heat when, dropped

For bread, children poke and lunge with sticks.
At midday, soup: picture hands that chop
The spinach, veal bones collapsing

With the cleaver brought down hard on wood.
At dawn, a man, asleep or drunk, rumpled
On the cloister wall: his clothes are ripped

And bloody like his hands. He flaunts his tongue
As lizards do while one clings to his knee,
And, motionless, does not gaze at the fruit

Or at the blackbirds, nestled in the glass.
They know, well-married to their world, the bitter
Taste of what is green and does not move.

Threshold of the Visible World

for Kaja Silverman

1.

So as children do, he began to learn
About the universe, rings and clouds
In order, every orbit, every asteroid

Predictable and lucid, and he knew
He'd calculate the sun's heat more precisely
If he climbed a hill to find his place

In the oppressive turning of each day.
How wrong it seemed that hills
Could make no difference in the universe,

Like standing on an onion skin to reach
The dull hum of long fluorescent lights.
He fled the glare and fumbled through a culvert,

Hardly wider than a sparrow's flight,
And reached so far the sinews pulled
In their sockets, and the water, muck, and light

Mixed perfectly within his skull replaced
The world with one of their own making—
Light spray of the waterfall beyond

The summit and the burly moss that held
His footprints till they blurred with water,
One hand resting on the crater's lip,

A bird's egg cradled in his palm before it fell
Forever, like a star, as if to illustrate
The happy day his life would come to nothing.

2.

On the day his life had come to nothing
He left the music on the desk unplayed.
By the time he recognized the world outside

The house was a speck in open sky,
Beyond rooftops, trees, and radio towers.
Each face he saw resembled his own.

At the edge of town condominiums
Gave way to farms. Then forests rose,
Uninhabited places the soul presumes,

In loneliness, to understand...
Grass hip-high across the prairie,
Wagon ruts descending to a pile of bones,

The last survivor with a corn-husk doll
And silver relish tray beneath her skirts,
Her parents apparitions in the snow.

A river appeared before him, raging, beautiful,
Too dangerous to cross. No tracks, no voices,
Nothing he couldn't imagine there except

A rowboat sunk to its gunnels in mud.
The steady, unguarded music of the rapids
Drifted past him as he gripped the oars,

And like a sparrow hawk ascending
In the glare, a thought occurred to him:
To spend his life in service of others.

3.

To spend one's life in service of others,
Ferrying the dead across the river of dreams,
Watching their children, would not be servitude.

Tonight the children wander aimlessly
Across new-mown lawn. A halo rings
The moon, illuminating their upturned faces

Singing in the dark. It is a song
Their mother never sang as she was working
In the garden, poplars dancing in

Sunlight and the tiny rows of parsley
Radiant against fresh-turned soil.
It is a tired song. It is like the sound

Of the mother's voice inside the child
Who will walk along some foreign street,
The river grumbling, meaningless,

Below the bridge, no stars, a little rain
Against the chimney pots. The child
Will remember nothing but the sound

Of water in the snow where she had strayed,
Alone, when all the natural world began
To flow like water, colder than water,

And each vague atom of light convened
Within the image of her mother's face,
The threshold of the visible world.

4.

At the threshold of the visible world,
Without shelter, without clothing or bread,
Beyond the magnitude of human voices

Or will to sing, or singing, to be heard,
A cloud appeared to cover the hill
In mysterious shade. The seasons changed.

The river shriveled back into its source
And in a single night, long duration
Of the planet's course of tilt and spin,

The pass between the mountain and the lake
Was lost before it ever could be found,
Noon a trickle of light, the chimney now

A blackened dimple in snow. Here
The mind forgets itself and cries out sharply
At the sight of angels in the clouds:

Hands reached down to fold her body
In a golden shawl, mushroom odor
Of death in the air as they rolled

The final pinch of crumbs together
With their own saliva in a ball
And pressed it gently to her lips.

Wingbeats, minnows of light in the shoals.
She broke the surface. But she wept to know
The undeniable existence of the stars.

5.

The undeniable existence of the stars
Is not mysterious, like guilt, the way
A woman wandering the halls at night

Washes her hands again and again
Although they are not dirty. I'm not free
To speculate on motives any further.

Once, when he was two or three, the world
Lay open to him, damp, unsupervised,
A silver net of snow-mold on the grass:

As his footprints disappeared, he thought
Of counting everything they left behind,
First rooftops, then the broken trees,

And as he did, the sound of human voices
Drifted steadily away from him
Until the world was all that he could hear.

I've learned the hard way that the mind
Has nothing on an oyster when it comes
To comprehending its own pearls,

That at its center is a corridor
Extending down to the unknown,
The sloppy escapade of consciousness,

In which the meshwork of desire rises
Undistinguished from its object
Like a mushroom out of its mycelium.

6.

Like a mushroom out of its mycelium
He'd reappear above the surface of the water
If the planet lurched to let him through.

No prospects from the summit so he walked
Along the frozen crust. A red flag tilted
In the distance, signaling a life

Below the surface, but it disappeared
The way bird song echoes in the brain.
Inventing systems he remained a part

Of systems till he walked so far he stumbled
On a frozen swan, the surface clear
Enough to show black feet dangling in

The current, the wilted beak, as if the body
Could be trapped beneath the skull,
Hands scraping drowsily against a sheath

Of bone that once was soft enough
To show the gentle pulsing of the brain.
He wondered how the image would appear

From shore, bright coat billowing
Across the surface and the gulls cascading,
Unaware. The pieces that compose

The pattern are not new. He realized
He knew nothing of the universe.
So as children do, he began to learn.

What If

What if I'd fallen through instead of driving here,
Where ransacked shelves belie our last abiding myth
Of plenitude, some carts half empty, others half full?

What if the moment when I floated free, suspended
Between two impenetrable planes of earth and sky,
Released some long forgotten memory that shattered
When I hit the ice?
                    Would I have bolted upright,
Brushed my coat as if dignity could outstrip pain
Although no one were watching but myself?
                                    If
For that moment I had glimpsed sunburnt palaces
Rising from the sea, rooftops breaking in marble foam,
All the ancient, volatile stabilities,

Would I have sacrificed the share of bland good luck
That is our sustenance, shelves stocked with everything
We need except the need, the hunger, our capacity
For easily forgotten happiness?

                              Who would have picked
These oranges? What knowledge could bring a sweetness
To my mouth more fleeting than the mind sustains
When the body can't distinguish thought from sense—
Each moment passing like a storm, no sign,
Making our death a matter of indifference?

Letting Go

The highest point for miles but it's nothing
Like the natural world. Too steep for vistas
So it's valueless as real estate. A rise
Of sumac, burning red—a scarecrow
Made of roots and mud collapsing slowly
At the last frontier of suburban sprawl.

There weren't tablets or a crater's rim
For Petrarch climbing Mont Ventoux,
His only obstacle the nature of the place.
At the summit Augustine rebuked him:
Men admire high mountains and great floods,
Wide-rolling rivers and the ring of ocean
And the movement of the stars—forgetting
Nothing is admirable except the soul.

It's not the wild grape leaves, figs and alders
On slopes around you or the terraced rows
Of olives, bleached to silver, down below;
It's not a sumac's fire, the city's rise
Of glass and steel or the polished surface
Of Ontario, just visible in winter
When the sycamores drop their leaves.

It's bed springs, one shoe littering the trail,
A condom near the black char of a fire
Ringed with stones, the man who shared
His blanket with a doberman or else
A worn out book you bring to scatter
Language at the top—anything
To guarantee there never were natural worlds
The soul kept alone.
                              It's like not being
Able to let go. The downtown pigeon
Jerking pizza crust from side to side
Because at home, a hundred years ago
On Adriatic cliffs, it fed on seed pods,
Shaking nature's handouts free.

The Lucky Ones

One by one leaves go limp and scatter
On the trout pond, a few of them escaping

Down the mossy sluice that separates
Whatever has been built here from the forest

With its tall scrim of dilapidated birch.
Unsuffered, all the years of letting go,

Houses and the children or the words
Of longing and regret that what we spoke,

A language almost foreign, never could
Accommodate. But as they skim across

The river to open shore, whatever sings
Most loudly in the rushes—everything

Unsaid, untouched, even undesired
In the life they gathered up before—

Is what the body will remember most
Tenaciously, what takes its place before

We're swindled free of everything we think
Of as ourselves, a leaf's arterial display.

The fish, mouths open, larger now,
All drive their sleek, long bodies

At the dark spot floating on the surface,
Thundering at once before they whip

Themselves into reverse. And even you,
One of the lucky ones, know only where

You've come from, nothing of the sunlit
Undecipherable air beyond the line.